The Selected Poems of
Irving Layton

The Selected Poems of

Irving
Layton

A NEW DIRECTIONS BOOK

Layton

Manufactured in the United States of America
First published clothbound and as New Directions Paperbook 431 in 1977

Library of Congress Cataloging in Publication Data

Layton, Irving, 1912–
    The selected poems of Irving Layton.
    (A New Directions Book)
    I. Title.
PR9199.3.L35A17   1977   811'.5'4   76–54704
ISBN 0–8112–0641–6
ISBN 0–8112–0642–4 pbk.

New Directions Books are published for James Laughlin
by New Directions Publishing Corporation,
333 Sixth Avenue, New York 10014

INTRODUCTION

Irving Layton is Canada's most prolific as well as most celebrated poet, and in thirty years he has issued some thirty volumes, which lately have been running to eighty poems apiece. Some of his poems are better than others, and Canadians who have lived with him for decades seem to take his habit of bundling the day's irritations into a poem for granted, like mosquitoes and imperfectly bilingual postmen. Readers elsewhere, making his acquaintance in a winnowed compilation, may double their pleasure in his best by reflecting that if his less good is missing from this volume, still it exists and has had its uses.

For the ephemeral poems do serve to keep the poet limber, and strewn through a Layton book they have value for a reader too, providing the noise from which the sonorities crystallize, making the successful poems when they happen seem random miracles like (on a cooling planet) the genesis of life.

Which is how they are meant to seem, as though just dashed off. Perhaps they are, perhaps not. Their genre anyhow is Blake's, Whitman's, Lawrence's, Williams's: that of the seeming improvisation. An example:

DIVINITY

Were I a clumsy poet
I'd compare you to Helen;
Ransack the mythologies
Greek, Chinese, and Persian

For a goddess vehement
And slim; one with form as fair.
Yet find none. O, Love, you are
Lithe as a Jew peddler

And full of grace. Such lightness
Is in your step, instruments
I keep for the beholder
To prove you walk, not dance.

Merely to touch you is fire
In my head; my hair becomes

A burning bush. When you speak,
Like Moses I am dumb

With marvelling, or like him
I stutter with pride and fear:
I hold, Love, divinity
In my changed face and hair.

All of this says, I stammer with wonder. The first line seems
unsure whether to stress *clumsy* or *poet*: I'm not a *clumsy* poet,
the kind that contrives comparisons when there aren't any; or,
I'm not a poet at all, I do without art. Either way, I'm simply
uttering what words I can, and as early as line six you can tell
I'm not counting syllables; as for "instruments" in the third
stanza, that's a nonce-word to be going on with. (What instru-
ments can he possibly have in mind? John Donne would have let
us know.) So the poem enacts its own sincerity: you reduce me
to doggerel, to bare halting talk. And yet –

And yet those quatrains are more than typographical: their
second and fourth lines all rhyme slantwise, the way Yeats
rhymes *stain* and *moon*, or *head* and *blood*. (This takes more of a
poet's concentration than exact rhyming, because the words
won't prompt one another the way *stain* does *slain*.) And in its
fourth and fifth stanzas this poem that began by rejecting liter-
ary talk is fetching its fire and its dumbness from Sappho (the "
"Phainetai moi" which Catullus also imitated) while allowing us
to notice only the burning bush from Exodus. (And the poet is
both the burning bush and Moses, both godlike and the god's
supplicant.) Do such things simply happen, when a poet is suffi-
ciently rapt? That's what the poem would have us believe.

Layton's art is always to sound artless, and maybe he is but
one needn't wholly believe it. His fine gift of Voltairean detach-
ment (see "The Cockroach") seems like something you could
keep up just by cocking your head the right way, though you'd
be unlikely to manage such a detail as "All the lovely, meaning-
ful things they had said to each other about cockroaches were
forgotten." His parables drawn from the vulnerability of animals
(see "Cain") have the transparency of folk-tales. His climaxes
are apt to explode in one-syllable words (see for instance the
much-quoted quatrain,

They dance best who dance with desire,
Who lifting feet of fire from fire

Weave before they lie down
A red carpet for the sun

from "For Mao Tse-Tung: A Meditation on Flies and Kings.")
He can seem to be just tossing words at the page –

> ... the anguished
> half-choked
> sputtering cry
> the circumscribed tide
> makes – its hiss
> and last sign –
> before it collapses
> on the white sand
> and dies

– and achieve the imitation of a spent wave's phantasmal sound
that has taunted poets to emulate it since Homer's *polyphloisboio
thalasse*. (Layton's lines are a detail from "Tide," a poem not
collected here. There's plenty of first-class Layton outside this
selection.)

What keeps all this going is prodigious physical energy and a
blustery defiance of Canada, where Layton has lived since he
was one year old (he was born, 1912, in Roumania). Canada
(Wyndham Lewis's "sanctimonious icebox") is an easy country
to defy, its satirizable institutions have so little fight –

> A dull people, without charm
> or ideas,
> settling into the clean empty look
> of a Mountie or dairy farmer
> as into a legacy

– and Layton being caustic about it is doing two-finger exercises;
that one is called "From Colony to Nation." But he owes it
much too that he's never pinned down: a sunlight like his harsh
ironic mind, an urban bustle that doesn't *engulf* in New York's
way or London's, an easy commerce with the undeveloped land
where for lack of barbered distances you may as well look
closely at snakes and frogs; most notably a milieu for the mind
that doesn't help a poet develop his idiom but, remote from any
workable poetic, doesn't jam his signals either. (In England,
Eliot found, the language needs viewing with "animosity," so

insidiously do its literary echoes wrest control away from the poet.)

Neither French nor British, Layton looks around him in Montreal with the eye of an exasperated alien (see "On Seeing the Statuettes of Ezekiel and Jeremiah in the Church of Notre Dame"). It was natural that he should have developed the poetic of the one-man show – *Balls for a One-Armed Juggler*, as the title of a 1963 collection has it. Each new poem, of hundreds on hundreds, tests out the performance anew. (One-armed jugglers need luck, and it only works sometimes.) Defining his expectations against those of the city's pervading religion, he hopes for little from man save cussedness, from woman save felicity, or from life save moments of lovely instinctual flowering. That its members might from time to time stumble into the momentary joy of being alive is the most he can find it in him to wish for the human race, bound as it is to a mortality it shares with flies and a disingenuous passion it shares with Hitler. The lover breaks free sometimes, and the poet when his poem works. Distrusting alike theophanies and meliorations, the poems hold out hope only for themselves: for rare transparencies accessible it may be only to poets and vicariously a little to the rest of us.

> Enough that we two can find
> A laughter in the mind
> For the interlocking grass
> The winds part as they pass;
> Or fallen on each other,
> Leaf and uprooted flower.

– Hugh Kenner.

THE SWIMMER

The afternoon foreclosing, see
The swimmer plunges from his raft,
Opening the spray corollas by his act of war –
The snake heads strike
Quickly and are silent.

Emerging see how for a moment
A brown weed with marvellous bulbs,
He lies imminent upon the water
While light and sound come with a sharp passion
From the gonad sea around the Poles
And break in bright cockle-shells about his ears.

He dives, floats, goes under like a thief
Where his blood sings to the tiger shadows
In the scentless greenery that leads him home,
A male salmon down fretted stairways
Through underwater slums. . . .

Stunned by the memory of lost gills
He frames gestures of self-absorption
Upon the skull-like beach;
Observes with instigated eyes
The sun that empties itself upon the water,
And the last wave romping in
To throw its boyhood on the marble sand.

PARACLETE

I have studied history, he said.
I expect nothing from man
Save hecatombs.
C'est son métier. And ferity.

No longer perhaps to his own kind
But to the sulphur-coloured butterfly
And young seals, white, without defence –
To whatever crawls, flies, swims.

It is life itself offends this queer beast
And fills him with mysterious unease;
Consequently only half-movements
Delight him – writhings, tortured spasms

Or whatever can stir his derision
By defect or ungainliness
Or, maimed, flutters from weakness like a bird:
Say, a noble falcon, with splintered wing.

It is as if, killing, he looked for answers
To his discontent among severed veins
And in the hot blood of the slain
Sought to inundate forever his self-horror

Or like a sodden idiot who plucks
A thrush from a willow, grief in her green hair,
Throttles it to uncover the root of its song.

Let the gods who made him, pity him.

IN THE MIDST OF MY FEVER

In the midst of my fever, large
        as Europe's pain,
The birds hopping on the blackened wires
        were instantly electrocuted;
Bullfrogs were slaughtered in large numbers
        to the sound of their own innocent thrummings;
The beautiful whores of the king
        found lovers and disappeared;
The metaphysician sniffed the thought before him
        like a wrinkled fruit;
And the envoys meeting on the sunny quay
        for once said the truth about the weather.
In the midst of this rich confusion, a miracle happened: someone
        quietly performed a good deed;
And the grey imperial lions, growling, carried
        the news in their jaws.
I heard them. So did Androcles.

O from the height of my fever, the sweat
    ran down my hairless limbs
Like the blood from the condemned patron
    of specially unlucky slaves. Then, O then
Great Caesar's legions halted before my troubled ear,
    Jacobean in Time's double exposure.
My brassy limbs stiffened
    like a trumpet blast; surely
The minutes now covered with gold-dust
    will in time
Drop birdlime upon the handsomest
    standard-bearer,
Caesar himself discover the exhaustible flesh,
    my lips
White with prophecy aver before him.
But the conqueror's lips are like pearls,
    and he hurls his javelin at the target sky.

In the depth of my gay fever, I saw my limbs
    like Hebrew letters
Twisted with too much learning. I was
Seer, sensualist, or fake ambassador; the tyrant
    who never lied
And cried like an infant after he'd had to
    to succour his people.
Then I disengaging my arm to bless,
In an eyeblink became the benediction
    dropped from the Roman's fingers;
Nudes, nodes, nodules, became all one,
    existence seamless and I
Crawling solitary upon the globe of marble
    waited for the footfall which never came.
And I thought of Time's wretches and of some
    dear ones not yet dead
And of Coleridge taking laudanum.

THE BIRTH OF TRAGEDY

And me happiest when I compose poems.
Love, power, the huzza of battle
are something, are much;
yet a poem includes them like a pool
water and reflection.
In me, nature's divided things –
tree, mould on tree –
have their fruition;
I am their core. Let them swap,
bandy, like a flame swerve
I am their mouth; as a mouth I serve.

And I observe how the sensual moths
big with odour and sunshine
dart into the perilous shrubbery;
or drop their visiting shadows
upon the garden I one year made
of flowering stone to be a footstool
for the perfect gods:
who, friends to the ascending orders,
sustain all passionate meditations
and call down pardons
for the insurgent blood.

A quite madman, never far from tears,
I lie like a slain thing
under the green air the trees
inhabit, or rest upon a chair
towards which the inflammable air
tumbles on many robins' wings;
noting how seasonably
leaf and blossom uncurl
and living things arrange their death,
while someone from afar off
blows birthday candles for the world

THE COLD GREEN ELEMENT

At the end of the garden walk
the wind and its satellite wait for me;
their meaning I will not know
                    until I go there,
but the black-hatted undertaker

who, passing, saw my heart beating in the grass,
is also going there. Hi, I tell him,
a great squall in the Pacific blew a dead poet
                    out of the water,
who now hangs from the city's gates.

Crowds depart daily to see it, and return
with grimaces and incomprehension;
if its limbs twitched in the air
                    they would sit at its feet
peeling their oranges.

And turning over I embrace like a lover
the trunk of a tree, one of those
for whom the lightning was too much
                    and grew a brilliant
hunchback with a crown of leaves.

The ailments escaped from the labels
of medicine bottles are all fled to the wind;
I've seen myself lately in the eyes
                    of old women,
spent streams mourning my manhood,

in whose old pupils the sun became
a bloodsmear on broad catalpa leaves
and hanging from ancient twigs,
                    my murdered selves
sparked the air like the muted collisions

13

of fruit. A black dog howls down my blood,
a black dog with yellow eyes;
he too by someone's inadvertence
                    saw the bloodsmear
on the broad catalpa leaves.

But the furies clear a path for me to the worm
who sang for an hour in the throat of a robin,
and misled by the cries of young boys
                    I am again
a breathless swimmer in that cold green element.

THE IMPROVED BINOCULARS

Below me the city was in flames:
the firemen were the first to save
themselves. I saw steeples fall on their knees.

I saw an agent kick the charred bodies
from an orphanage to one side, marking
the site carefully for a future speculation.

Lovers stopped short of the final spasm
and went off angrily in opposite directions,
their elbows held by giant escorts of fire.

Then the dignitaries rode across the bridges
under an auricle of light which delighted them,
noting for later punishment those that went before.

And the rest of the populace, their mouths
distorted by an unusual gladness, bawled thanks
to this comely and ravaging ally, asking

Only for more light with which to see
their neighbour's destruction.

All this I saw through my improved binoculars.

SONG FOR NAOMI

Who is that in the tall grasses singing
By herself, near the water?
I can not see her
But can it be her
Than whom the grasses so tall
Are taller,
My daughter,
My lovely daughter?

Who is that in the tall grasses running
Beside her, near the water?
She can not see there
Time that pursued her
In the deep grasses so fast
And faster
And caught her,
My foolish daughter.

What is the wind in the fair grass saying
Like a verse, near the water?
Saviours that over
All things have power
Make Time himself grow kind
And kinder
That sought her,
My little daughter.

Who is that at the close of the summer
Near the deep lake? Who wrought her
Comely and slender?
Time but attends and befriends her
Than whom the grasses though tall
Are not taller,
My daughter,
My gentle daughter.

CHOKECHERRIES

The sun's gift –

but the leaves a sickly green;
the more exposed curling, showing
a bleached white, many with ragged
holes;
Caterpillars have been
here
sliding their slow destructive bodies
over them.

I think of them, the leaves, as hoplites
or as anything ingloriously
useful,
suffering, dying . . .

But the chokecherries,
ah;
Still, the leaves' sacrifice
is acrid on the tongue.

GOLFERS

Like Sieur Montaigne's distinction
between virtue and innocence
what gets you is their unbewilderment

They come into the picture suddenly
like unfinished houses, gapes and planed wood,
dominating a landscape

And you see at a glance
among sportsmen they are the metaphysicians,
intent, untalkative, pursuing Unity

(What finally gets you is their chastity)

And that no theory of pessimism is complete
which altogether ignores them

WHATEVER ELSE POETRY IS FREEDOM

Whatever else poetry is freedom.
Forget the rhetoric, the trick of lying
All poets pick up sooner or later. From the river,
Rising like the thin voice of grey castratos – the mist;
Poplars and pines grow straight but oaks are gnarled;
Old codgers must speak of death, boys break windows;
Women lie honestly by their men at last.

And I who gave my Kate a blackened eye
Did to its vivid changing colours
Make up an incredible musical scale;
And now I balance on wooden stilts and dance
And thereby sing to the loftiest casements.
See how with polish I bow from the waist.
Space for these stilts! More space or I fail!

And a crown I say for my buffoon's head.
Yet no more fool am I than King Canute,
Lord of our tribe, who scanned and scorned;
Who half-deceived, believed; and, poet, missed
The first white waves come nuzzling at his feet;
Then damned the courtiers and the foolish trial
With a most bewildering and unkingly jest.

It was the mist. It lies inside one like a destiny.
A real Jonah it lies rotting like a lung.
And I know myself undone who am a clown
And wear a wreath of mist for a crown;
Mist with the scent of dead apples,
Mist swirling from black oily waters at evening,
Mist from the fraternal graves of cemeteries.

It shall drive me to beg my food and at last
Hurl me broken I know and prostrate on the road;
Like a huge toad I saw, entire but dead,
That Time mordantly had blacked; O pressed
To the moist earth it pled for entry.
I shall be I say that stiff toad for sick with mist
And crazed I smell the odour of mortality.

17

And Time flames like a paraffin stove
And what it burns are the minutes I live.
At certain middays I have watched the cars
Bring me from afar their windshield suns;
What lay to my hand were blue fenders,
The suns extinguished, the drivers wearing sunglasses.
And it made me think I had touched a hearse.

So whatever else poetry is freedom. Let
Far off the impatient cadences reveal
A padding for my breathless stilts. Swivel,
O hero, in the fleshy groves, skin and glycerine,
And sing of lust, the sun's accompanying shadow
Like a vampire's wing, the stillness in dead feet –
Your stave brings resurrection, O aggrievèd king.

MISUNDERSTANDING

I placed
my hand
upon
her thigh.

By the way
she moved
away
I could see
her devotion
to literature
was not
perfect.

ON SEEING THE STATUETTES OF
EZEKIEL AND JEREMIAH IN
THE CHURCH OF NOTRE DAME

They have given you French names
     and made you captive, my rugged
troublesome compatriots;
     your splendid beards, here, are epicene,
plaster white
       and your angers
unclothed with Palestinian hills quite lost
in this immense and ugly edifice.

You are bored – I see it – sultry prophets
     with priests and nuns
(What coarse jokes must pass between you!)
     and with those morbidly religious
i.e. my prize brother-in-law
       ex-Lawrencian
pawing his rosary, and his wife
sick with many guilts.

Believe me I would gladly take you
     from this spidery church
its bad melodrama, its musty smell of candle
     and set you both free again
in no make-believe world
       of sin and penitence
but the sunlit square opposite
alive at noon with arrogant men.

Yet cheer up Ezekiel and you Jeremiah
     who were once cast into a pit;
I shall not leave you here incensed, uneasy
     among alien Catholic saints
but shall bring you from time to time
     my hot Hebrew heart
as passionate as your own, and stand
with you here awhile in aching confraternity.

FAMILY PORTRAIT

That owner of duplexes
has enough gold to sink himself
on a battleship. His children,
two sons and a daughter, are variations
on the original gleam: that is,
    slobs with a college education.

Right now the four of them
are seated in the hotel's dining-room
munching watermelons.

With the assurance of money
in the bank
they spit out the black, cool, elliptical
melonseeds, and you can tell
the old man has rocks
but no culture: he spits,
    gives the noise away free.

The daughter however is embarrassed
(Second Year Arts, McGill) and sucks harder
to forget.

They're about as useless
as tits on a bull,
and I think:
"Thank heaven I'm not
Jesus Christ –
I don't have to love them."

CAIN

Taking the air rifle from my son's hand,
I measured back five paces, the Hebrew
In me, narcissist, father of children,
Laid to rest. From there I took aim and fired.
The silent ball hit the frog's back an inch
Below the head. He jumped at the surprise
Of it, suddenly tickled or startled
(He must have thought) and leaped from the wet sand
Into the surrounding brown water. But
The ball had done its mischief. His next spring
Was a miserable flop, the thrust all gone
Out of his legs. He tried – like Bruce – again,
Throwing out his sensitive pianist's
Hands as a dwarf might or a helpless child.
His splash disturbed the quiet pondwater
And one old frog behind his weedy moat
Blinking, looking self-complacently on.
The lin's surface at once became closing
Eyelids and bubbles like notes of music
Liquid, luminous, dropping from the page
White, white-bearded, a rapid crescendo
Of inaudible sounds and a crones' whispering
Backstage among the reeds and bulrushes
As for an expiring Lear or Oedipus.

But Death makes us all look ridiculous.
Consider this frog (dog, hog, what you will)
Sprawling, his absurd corpse rocked by the tides
That his last vain spring had set in movement.
Like a retired oldster, I couldn't help sneer,
Living off the last of his insurance:
Billows – now crumbling – the premiums paid.

Absurd, how absurd. I wanted to kill
At the mockery of it, kill and kill
Again – the self-infatuate frog, dog, hog,
Anything with the stir of life in it,
Seeing the dead leaper, Chaplin-footed,
Rocked and cradled in this afternoon
Of tranquil water, reeds, and blazing sun,

The hole in his back clearly visible
And the torn skin a blob of shadow
Moving when the quiet poolwater moved.
O Egypt, marbled Greece, resplendent Rome,
Did you also finally perish from a small bore
In your back you could not scratch? And would
Your mouths open ghostily, gasping out
Among the murky reeds, the hidden frogs,
We climb with crushed spines toward the heavens?

When the next morning I came the same way
The frog was on his back, one delicate
Hand on his belly, and his white shirt front
Spotless. He looked as if he might have been
A comic; tapdancer apologizing
For a fall, or an Emcee, his wide grin
Coaxing a laugh from us for an aside
Or perhaps a joke we didn't quite hear.

BUTTERFLY ON ROCK

The large yellow wings, black-fringed,
were motionless

They say the soul of a dead person
will settle like that on the still face

But I thought: the rock has borne this;
this butterfly is the rock's grace,
its most obstinate and secret desire
to be a thing alive made manifest

Forgot were the two shattered porcupines
I had seen die in the bleak forest.
Pain is unreal; death, an illusion:
There is no death in all the land,
I heard my voice cry;
And brought my hand down on the butterfly
And felt the rock move beneath my hand.

FOR MAO TSE-TUNG:
A MEDITATION ON FLIES AND KINGS

So, circling about my head, a fly.
Haloes of frantic monotone.
Then a smudge of blood smoking
On my fingers, let Jesus and Buddha cry.

Is theirs the way? Forgiveness of hurt?
Leprosariums? Perhaps. But I
Am burning flesh and bone,
An indifferent creature between
Cloud and a stone;
Smash insects with my boot,
Feast on torn flowers, deride
The nonillion bushes by the road
(Their patience is very great.)
Jivatma, they endure,
Endure and proliferate.

And the meek-browed and poor
In their solid tenements
(Etiolated, they do not dance.)
Worry of priest and of commissar:
None may re-create them who are
Lowly and universal as the moss
Or like vegetation the winds toss
Sweeping to the open lake and sky.
I put down these words in blood
And would not be misunderstood:
They have their Christs and their legends
And out of their pocks and ailments
Weave dear enchantments –
Poet and dictator, you are as alien as I.

On this remote and classic lake
Only the lapsing of the water can I hear
And the cold wind through the sumac.
The moneyed and their sunburnt children
Swarm other shores. Here is ecstasy,
The sun's outline made lucid
By each lacustral cloud
And man naked with mystery.

They dance best who dance with desire,
Who lifting feet of fire from fire
Weave before they lie down
A red carpet for the sun.

I pity the meek in their religious cages
And flee them; and flee
The universal sodality
Of joy-haters, joy-destroyers
(O Schiller, wine-drunk and silly!)
The sufferers and their thick rages;
Enter this tragic forest where the trees
Uprear as if for the graves of men,
All function and desire to offend
With themselves finally done;
And mark the dark pines farther on,
The sun's fires touching them at will,
Motionless like silent khans
Mourning serene and terrible
Their Lord entombed in the blazing hill.

BERRY PICKING

Silently my wife walks on the still wet furze
Now darkgreen the leaves are full of metaphors
Now lit up is each tiny lamp of blueberry.
The white nails of rain have dropped and the sun is free.

And whether she bends or straightens to each bush
To find the children's laughter among the leaves
Her quiet hands seem to make the quiet summer hush –
Berries or children, patient she is with these.

I only vex and perplex her; madness, rage
Are endearing perhaps put down upon the page;
Even silence daylong and sullen can then
Enamour as restraint or classic discipline.

So I envy the berries she puts in her mouth.
The red and succulent juice that stains her lips;
I shall never taste that good to her, nor will they
Displease her with a thousand barbarous jests.

How they lie easily for her hand to take,
Part of the unoffending world that is hers;
Here beyond complexity she stands and stares
And leans her marvellous head as if for answers.

No more the easy soul my childish craft deceives
Nor the simpler one for whom yes is always yes;
No, now her voice comes to me from a far way off
Though her lips are redder than the raspberries.

DIVINITY

Were I a clumsy poet
I'd compare you to Helen;
Ransack the mythologies
Greek, Chinese, and Persian

For a goddess vehement
And slim; one with form as fair.
Yet find none. O, love, you are
Lithe as a Jew peddler

And full of grace. Such lightness
Is in your step, instruments
I keep for the beholder
To prove you walk, not dance.

Merely to touch you is fire
In my head; my hair becomes
A burning bush. When you speak,
Like Moses I am dumb

With marvelling, or like him
I stutter with pride and fear:
I hold, Love, divinity
In my changed face and hair.

25

KEINE LAZAROVITCH
1870-1959

When I saw my mother's head on the cold pillow,
Her white waterfalling hair in the cheeks' hollows,
I thought, quietly circling my grief, of how
She had loved God but cursed extravagantly his creatures.

For her final mouth was not water but a curse,
A small black hole, a black rent in the universe,
Which damned the green earth, stars and trees in its stillness
And the inescapable lousiness of growing old.

And I record she was comfortless, vituperative,
Ignorant, glad, and much else besides; I believe
She endlessly praised her black eyebrows, their thick weave,
Till plagiarizing Death leaned down and took them for his mould.

And spoiled a dignity I shall not again find,
And the fury of her stubborn limited mind.
Now none will shake her amber beads and call God blind,
Or wear them upon a breast so radiantly.

O fierce she was, mean and unaccommodating;
But I think now of the toss of her gold earrings,
Their proud carnal assertion, and her youngest sings
While all the rivers of her red veins move into the sea.

A TALL MAN EXECUTES A JIG

I

So the man spread his blanket on the field
And watched the shafts of light between the tufts
And felt the sun push the grass towards him;
The noise he heard was that of whizzing flies,
The whistlings of some small imprudent birds,
And the ambiguous rumbles of cars
That made him look up at the sky, aware
Of the gnats that tilted against the wind
And in the sunlight turned to jigging motes.
Fruitflies he'd call them except there was no fruit
About, spoiling to hatch these glitterings,
These nervous dots for which the mind supplied
The closing sentences from Thucydides,
Or from Euclid having a savage nightmare.

II

Jig jig, jig jig. Like minuscule black links
Of a chain played with by some playful
Unapparent hand or the palpitant
Summer haze bored with the hour's stillness.
He felt the sting and tingle afterwards
Of those leaving their orthodox unrest,
Leaving their undulant excitation
To drop upon his sleeveless arm. The grass,
Even the wildflowers became black hairs
And himself a maddened speck among them.
Still the assaults of the small flies made him
Glad at last, until he saw purest joy
In their frantic jiggings under a hair,
So changed from those in the unrestraining air.

III

He stood up and felt himself enormous.
Felt as might Donatello over stone,
Or Plato, or as a man who has held
A loved and lovely woman in his arms
And feels his forehead touch the emptied sky
Where all antinomies flood into light.

Yet jig jig jig, the haloing black jots
Meshed with the wheeling fire of the sun:
Motion without meaning, disquietude
Without sense or purpose, ephermerides
That mottled the resting summer air till
Gusts swept them from his sight like wisps of smoke.
Yet they returned, bring a bee who, seeing
But a tall man, left him for a marigold.

IV

He doffed his aureole of gnats and moved
Out of the field as the sun sank down,
A dying god upon the blood-red hills.
Ambition, pride, the ecstasy of sex,
And all circumstance of delight and grief,
That blood upon the mountain's side, that flood
Washed into a clear incredible pool
Below the ruddied peaks that pierced the sun.
He stood still and waited. If ever
The hour of revelation was come
It was now, here on the transfigured steep.
The sky darkened. Some birds chirped. Nothing else.
He thought the dying god had gone to sleep:
An Indian fakir on his mat of nails.

V

And on the summit of the asphalt road
Which stretched towards the fiery town, the man
Saw one hill raised like a hairy arm, dark
With pines and cedars against the stricken sun
– The arm of Moses or of Joshua.
He dropped his head and let fall the halo
Of mountains, purpling and silent as time,
To see temptation coiled before his feet:
A violated grass snake that lugged
Its intestine like a small red valise.
A cold-eyed skinflint it now was, and not
The manifest of that joyful wisdom,
The mirth and arrogant green flame of life;
Or earth's vivid tongue that flicked in praise of earth.

VI

And the man wept because pity was useless.
"Your jig's up; the flies come like kites," he said
And watched the grass snake crawl towards the hedge,
Convulsing and dragging into the dark
The satchel filled with curses for the earth,
For the odours of warm sedge, and the sun,
A blood-red organ in the dying sky.
Backwards it fell into a grassy ditch
Exposing its underside, white as milk,
And mocked by wisps of hay between its jaws;
And then it stiffened to its final length.
But though it opened its thin mouth to scream
A last silent scream that shook the black sky,
Adamant and fierce, the tall man did not curse.

VII

Beside the rigid snake the man stretched out
In fellowship of death; he lay silent
And still in the heavy grass with eyes shut,
Inhaling the moist odours of the night
Through which his mind tunnelled with flicking tongue
Backwards to caves, mounds, and sunken ledges
And desolate cliffs where comes only kites,
And where of perished badgers and racoons
The claws alone remain, gripping the earth.
Meanwhile the green snake crept upon the sky,
Huge, his mailed coat glittering with stars that made
The night bright, and blowing thin wreaths of cloud
Athwart the moon; and as the weary man
Stood up, coiled above his head, transforming all.

THE CAGE

I turn away to hide my terror
Lest my unmanliness displease them
And maim for all a half-holiday
Begun so well, so auspiciously.
They are building the mythical cage
Whose slow rise allows janitors, whores,
And bank presidents to display love
To one another like a curious
Wound: the Elect to undertake feats
Of unusual virtue. Masons
Give stone and ironmongers, metal
As if these were forever useless
In a paradise of leaves and sun;
And a blacksmith, handsome and selfless,
Offers to blind me at once without
Charge. A quiet shiver of self-love,
Of self-approbation runs through each
At the discovery of so much
Altruism – unknown, hitherto,
Unsuspected – in their very midst.
The instance of the meek stonemasons,
The ironmongers and the selfless blacksmith
Seizes like a panic. Suddenly
Each one vies with his neighbour, avid
To seek out the more burdensome toil:
This one lugging spikes; that one, planks.
Affecting it is to watch their grace,
Their fine courtesies to each other
When they collide; or to imagine
Their tenderness in bed when they leave
The square littered with balloons and me
Blinded and raging in this huge cage.

WITH THE MONEY I SPEND

With the money I spend on you
I could buy ice cream for Korean kings.
I could adopt a beggar
        and clothe him in scarlet and gold
I could leave a legacy of dolls and roses
            to my grandchildren.
Why must you order expensive Turkish cigarettes?
And why do you drink only the most costly champagne?
The Leninists are marching on us.
Their eyes are inflamed with social justice.
Their mouths are contorted with the brotherhood of man.
Their fists are heavy with universal love.
They have not read a line of Mayakovsky's poems
        for twelve whole months.
The deprivation has made them desperate.
With staring eyeballs they hold off
        waiting for the ash from your cigarette to fall.
That is the signal.
When the ash crumbles, the man with the smallest forehead
        will smash a cracked hourglass, the sound
            amplified into a thousand manifestos.
Can you not see them? Can you not hear them?
Already they are closing in on us.
Your fragrant body means nothing to them.
Under your very eyes, velvet and remarkable,
        they intone that Beauty is not absolute.
They shout for an unobstructed view of your shoulders,
        your proud and beautiful head gone.
They will break your arms and slender legs
        into firewood.
The golden delicate hairs I have kissed
        into fire a thousand times
            will blaze more brightly;
But who will bend down to gather the flames
        into their mouth?
Who will follow their white light into eternity?
Because I love you better
        than artichokes and candles in the dark,
I shall speak to them.
Perhaps they will overlook your grace for my sake,
        ignore the offending perfection of your lips.

Perhaps, after all, you and I will start
    a mass conversion into elegance.
I will tell them my father made cheese
    and was humble and poor all his life,
And that his father before him turned ill
    at the mere sight of money;
And that a certain remote ancestor of mine
    never saw money at all,
        having been born blind.
On my mother's side, they were all failures.
Calliopes will sound for my undistinguished lineage
And the aroused Leninists will at once guess
    I am a fool in love, a simpleton,
        an ensnared and deranged proletarian
With no prospects but the wind which exposes
    my terrible hungers to them,
My counter-revolutionary appetite to be lost
    from all useful labour
        in your arms hair thighs navel;
And parting the clouds, one solitary star
    to show them where I am slain
Counting the gold coins
    for your Turkish cigarettes and costly champagne.

THE WELL-WROUGHT URN

"What would you do
if I suddenly died?"

"Write a poem to you."

"Would you mourn for me?"

"Certainly," I sighed.

"For a long time?"

"That depends."

"On what?"

"The poem's excellence," I replied.

32

ELEGY FOR MARILYN MONROE

Last summer, it was "Papa" Hemingway
This summer it's Marilyn Monroe
Next summer, who? – Who will it be?
But Orville Faubus gets re-elected
Two hundred million X-Laxed Americans
     go on defecating as before
and Congress acts as if nothing has happened

How come I asked of Lyndon Johnson
     there's no Committee
to investigate
the high rate of suicide
among those with a tragic overplus
of sensitivity and consciousness;
and received a postcard
     showing a Texan oil field.

Gentlemen, take it for what it's worth
but I suspect something more terrible
     than radioactive fallout
or the unmentionable gases of Belsen
has penetrated our human atmosphere.
The P.T.A.'s haven't heard of it yet
or the Board of Directors of Bell Tel
or President Kennedy;
moreover if I manoeuvred to let them know
     what it is
there'd be a Congressional committee
to investigate me!
They'd get cracking at once. O yes.

You ask, what is it
that goes straight for its victims like radar?
I name it the Zed-factor,
lethal only to the passionate, the imaginative,
     and to whatever is rare and delightful
in this brute universe.

Invisible as halitosis or body odour
it makes no warning of its presence;
therefore no T.V. outfit
will sing commercials to it
with chuckling hooligans

poking fingers through plugged drains,
and anyhow since only an infinitesimal part
of the nation
is susceptible to attack
why bother? See, why bother?

Good-bye Marilyn
It's raining in Magog
    a town you probably never heard of
where I sit in a tavern writing this;
nor did you ever hear of me
though I once composed a whole poem to you
and called you "Earth Goddess".
The janitors to whom you said hello,
the cabbies who spotted you by your stride
    and magnificent blonde hair
and whistled and honked their horns
to let you know their good luck,
the men all around the world
who touched your limbs in irreverent sleep
will miss your wiggle and crazy laugh,
but no one more than I
dazed this afternoon by grief and drink;
for I loved you from the first
who know what they do not know,
seeing in your death a tragic portent
for all of us who crawl and die
under the wheeling, disappearing stars;
and who must now live with the self-complacent,
    the enduring dull,
without your sustaining radiance,
your rarity.

From here on in
they have it, the pygmies have it,
it's all theirs!

Good-bye Marilyn
Sleep, sleep peacefully tonight
One poet at least will remember
    your brightness,
the unique fever in your form and face
(O insuperable filament, now black, now ash!)
and love you always.

EL GUSANO

From the place where I was sitting
I watched the weary stone-splitters
Building a road to blot out the sun;
And seeing their sweating bodies
In the merciless, mid-day heat
I wished I could do it for them:
Turn it out like a light, I mean.
And I almost rose up to do so
When my eyes suddenly picked out
A strange, never-before-seen worm
Making its way on the dried leaves.
It had a rich, feudal colour,
Reddish-brown like the Spanish soil
And knew its way among the stones
So plentiful in Alicante.
I love lizards and toads; spiders, too
And all humped and skin-crinkled creatures
But most in love I am with worms.
These sages never ask to know
A man's revenue or profession;
And it's not at antecedents
Or at class that they draw their line
But will dine with impartial relish
On one who splits stones or sells fish
Or, if it comes to that, a prince
Or a generalissimo.
Bless the subversive, crawling dears
Who here are the sole underground
And keep alive in the country
The idea of democracy.
I gave it a mock-Falangist
Salute and it crawled away; or
Was it the stone-splitters frightened
The worm off and the brittle noise
Of almond-pickers? It vanished
Under a dusty dried-up leaf
For a restful snooze in the ground
But I imagine it now tunnelling
Its hard way to Andalusia

Faithful to the colourful soil
Under the villas and motels
Of those whose bankers let them stow
Ancient distinctions and treasure
In the rear of their foreign cars.

O plundered, sold-out, and lovely
Shore of the Mediterranean:
This worm shall knit the scattered plots
Of your traduced, dismembered land;
And co-worker of wave and wind,
Proud, untiring apostle to
The fragrant and enduring dust,
Carry its political news
To Castile and to Aragon.

RHINE BOAT TRIP

The castles on the Rhine
are all haunted
by the ghosts of Jewish mothers
looking for their ghostly children

And the clusters of grapes
in the sloping vineyards
are myriads of blinded eyes
staring at the blind sun

The tireless Lorelei
can never comb from their hair
the crimson beards
of murdered rabbis

However sweetly they sing
one hears only
the low wailing of cattle-cars
moving invisibly across the land

MAHOGANY RED

Once, a single hair could bind me to you;
had you told me: "Jump
from the tallest building"
I'd have raced up on three elevators
and come down on my skull;
from the land of wailing ghosts
I'd have mailed you a fragment of skullbone
initialled by other desperate men
who had despaired of ever pleasing their lovers
Once, pleasure expanded in my phallus
like a thin, excruciating column of mercury;
when it exploded in by brain
it was like a movie I once saw
where the earth is grabbed by the sun
and fried black;
or another ice age arrived on snow
and I danced hot and bare and alone
on a lost glacier,
hairy mammoths circling around me.
Once, I was a galley-slave
lying stripped in all your fragrant ports;
a tickle in my groin
made your skin a torment to me,
and I dived into the dimples of your knees
when you stretched naked and sexy on your bed.
Godhead, the Marxist revolution, History
that is so full of tombs and tears,
I stuffed them all up your golden rectum
and sewed up their sole escape route
with frantic kisses sharper than needles.

Now, without warning
you are a middle-aged woman
who has tinted her hair mahogany red;
one of your front teeth, I notice, is discoloured grey;
I note, too, how often you say
"phony" and "artificial"
and wonder each time if you're not projecting;

—Yes, suddenly you are a woman
no different from other women;
a little less nasty perhaps,
a little less insincere,
less contemptuous of the male sex,
wistful and dissatisfied in your contempt,
still hankering for greatness, the dominant man,
his flowing locks all the spread-out sky you want,
unfair, conscienceless, your bag of woman's tricks close by,
hard beset, as women in all ages have been,
needing to make your way, to survive,
to be praised immoderately,
to be nibbled by a lover's amorous teeth,
to procreate . . .
vain of your seductive wiggle when you walk away from me,
of your perfect breasts displaying nipples
I wanted to devour
and die choking, their pink tips tickling my throat
vain of the fiery pennant under your chin
pinned there by your latest lover.

The bulb in my brain
once ignited and kept aglow
by genital electricity
lies smashed to bits.
I look out at the world with cool, aware eyes;
I pick out the pieces of grey glass from my brain;
I hold them all in my trembling hand.
Only a god could put them together again
and make them light up with sexual ecstasy,
but he lies sewn up in your golden rectum
huddled beside History and the Marxist revolution,
It is sad to be an atheist,
sadder yet to be one with a limp phallus.
Who knows
maybe if I had swung and knocked out
your one discoloured tooth
I would still love you, your little girl's grin,
small gap in your jaw
(who knows, who knows)
and not have wanted to write
this bitter, inaccurate poem.

AN OLD NICOISE WHORE

The famous and rich, even the learned and wise,
    Singly or in pairs went to her dwelling
To press their civilized lips to her thighs
    Or learn at first hand her buttocks' swelling.

Of high-paying customers she had no lack
    And was herself now rich: so she implied.
Mostly she had made her pile while on her back
    But sometimes she had made it on the side.

Reich she read; of course the Viennese doctor.
    Lawrence – his poems and novels she devoured;
Kafka at the beginning almost rocked her
    But as she read him more she said he soured.

Swedish she spoke, French, Polish, fluent German;
    Had even picked up Hindi – who knows how?
In bed she had learned to moan and sigh in Russian
    Though its rhythms troubled her even now.

A nymphomaniac like Napoleon's sister
    She could exhaust a bull or stallion;
Bankers had kneeled before her crotch to kiss her
    And ex-princes, Spanish and Italian.

And all the amorous mayors of France-Sud
    Impelled by lust or by regional pride
Would drive their Renaults into her neighborhood,
    Ring her bell and troop happily inside.

And pimpled teen-agers whom priests and rabbis
    Had made gauche, fearful, prurient and blind
Prodded by Venus had sought her expert thighs:
    Ah, to these she was especially kind.

And having translated several Swinburne lines
    She kept the finest whips she could afford
To be, though most aristocrats brought their canes,
    Ready for some forgetful English lord.

We saw waves like athletes dash towards the shore
    Breaking it seemed from a line of green scum;
We saw the sun dying, and this aged whore
    Noted how it gave clouds a tinge of rhum.

Engaging was her mien, her voice low and sweet;
    Convent nuns might have envied her address.
She was touched by the bathers below her feet;
    I, by this vitality sprung from cess.

And as she spoke to me on the crowded quay
    And reminisced about her well-spent years
I mourned with her her shrivelled face and body
    And gave what no man had given her: tears.

ELEGY FOR STRUL

Shall I be maliciously funny, Strul,
and say you look like a display of glassware
on crisp hospital sheets as white as yourself?
You who were once a barrel-chested
Mephistopheles
tempting a boy
to follow him down a pedlar's road
with adventure stories
of money and success;
a whoring, roaring bull of a man
that kicked up his heels
in my mother's kitchen
and filled our ears
with strange Balzacian tales
of priests and nuns:
better known in the villages, you boasted,
than Jesus himself
whose girls you fucked and afterwards tucked
a cheap medallion into their raw hands.

(But you were no cynic.
Life, you said, is a feed and a fart;
nor did terror make you a hypocrite.)

I hear sounds tumble out
from your cancered throat
and I bend down to your perishing mouth
to catch the dreadful whisper:
I lived like a fool, I am dying like one.
There are tears in my eyes
for you, Strul
– ogre of stinginess I once hated so much
but not now, lying there and dying.

(Where's the booming, unmalicious laugh
that belied the meanness
that made you run like a madman
switching off lights everywhere
and leaving your wife's guests in darkness?)

Now I see only your wasted physique
time and bugs have diminished
and the fantastic vitality
it once housed
ebbing into the surrounding space
minute by minute,
a mere pulse on the pillow . . .
a flutter . . .
and then you are still for ever,
only the wan tubes in your veins stirring
and catching the quiet light from the window.

THE HAUNTING

Why without cease do I think of a bold youth
        national origin unimportant or racial Peruvian
Russian Irish Javanese he has fine clear eyes
honest smiling mouth a pat for a child's head
talks to old women and helps them cross the street
        is friendly with mainliners anarchs and nuns
Cote St. Luc housewives their ruined husbands and brats
optometrists sign painters lumpenproletarians dumping
their humps into coffee cups plotting revenge
and clerics who've made out of Christ a bearded faggot

From the rotating movement of a girl's beautiful
     buttocks he draws energy as from the sun
(O lovely revolving suns on St. Catherine street)
and from breasts and perfumed shoulders and hair
Picadilly Wilhelmstrasse Fifth Avenue Rue St. Germain
     the suns go rolling on luminous hoops pinwheels
handsprings and somersaults of desirable flesh
the bold youth with wide-apart happy eyes
stepping lightly over blossoming asphalt graves is running
after them touching a child's head smiling to old women

Why don't I ever meet him face to face?
     sometimes I've seen him stepping off a bus
but when I've caught up with him he's changed
into a bourgeois giving the two-fingered peace sign
or a poet shouting love as if it were a bomb
     on damp days into an office clerk smelling of papers
is he somebody's doppelganger? an emanation or
shadow I see taking shape near a plateglass window?
who is he? he haunts me like an embodied absence
and as if I had lived all my life in arrears

ISRAELIS

It is themselves they trust and no one else;
Their fighter planes that screech across the sky,
Real, visible as the glorious sun;
Riflesmoke, gunshine, and rumble of tanks.

Man is a fanged wolf, without compassion
Or ruth: Assyrians, Medes, Greeks, Romans,
And devout pagans in Spain and Russia
– Allah's children, most merciful of all.

Where is the Almighty if murder thrives?
He's dead as mutton and they buried him
Decades ago, covered him with their own
Limp bodies in Belsen and Babi Yar.

Let the strong compose hymns and canticles,
Live with the Lord's radiance in their hard skulls
Or make known his great benevolences;
Stare at the heavens and feel glorified

42

Or humbled and awestruck buckle their knees:
They are done with him now and forever.
Without a whimper from him they returned,
A sign like an open hand in the sky.

The pillar of fire: Their flesh made it;
It burned briefly and died – you all know where.
Now in their own blood they temper the steel,
God being dead and their enemies not.

SHAKESPEARE

My young son asks me:
"who's the greatest poet?"
Without any fuss I say, Shakespeare
"Is he greater than you?"
I ho-ho around that one
and finally give a hard "yes."
"Will you ever be greater
than . . . a splatter of lisped S's
and P's . . . ?"
I look up at my son
from the page I'm writing on:
he too wants his answer
about the greatness of Shakespeare
though only six and carefree;
and I see with an amused hurt
how my son has begun to take on
one of those damned eternal fixtures
of the human imagination
like "God" or "Death" or "the start
of the world"; along with these
it'll be with him the rest
of his life like the birthmark
on his right buttock; so as though
I were explaining God or Death
I say firmly without a trace
of ho-ho in my voice: No, I'll never
be greater than William Shakespeare,
the world's greatest poetic genius
that ever will be or ever wuz

hoping my fair-minded admission
won't immediately blot out
the my-father-can-lick-anyone image
in his happy ignorant mind
and take the shine away
that's presently all around my head.
That unclimbable mountain, I rage;
that forever unapproachable star
pulsing its eternal beams from a far
stillness onto our narrow screens
set up as Palomar libraries and schools
to catch the faintest throb of light.
Damn that unscalable pinnacle
of excellence mocking our inevitable
inferiority and failure
like an obscene finger; a loud curse
on the jeering "beep . . . beeps"
that come from dark silence
and outer galactic space to unscramble
into the resonant signature of
"Full many a glorious morning" or
"The quality of mercy is not strained"
or "Out, out, brief candle . . . "
NO poet for all time, NO poet
till this planet crack into black night
and racking whirlwinds EVER
to be as great as William Shakespeare?
My God, what a calamitous burden
far worse than any horla or incubus:
a tyrant forever beyond the relief
of bullet or pointed steel . . .
What a terrible lion in one's path!
What a monumental stone
in the constrictive runnel of anyone
with an itch to write great poems
– and poets so cursed beyond all
by vanity, so loused up in each inch
of their angry, comfortless skin
with the intolerable twitch of envy!
Well, there's nothing to be done
about that bastard's unsurpassable
greatness; one accepts it like cancer
or old age, as something that one

must live with, hoping it will prod us on
to alertest dodges of invention
and circumvention, like the brave spider
who weaves his frail home in the teeth
of the lousiest storm and catches
the morning sun's approving smile;
Anyhow there's one saving grace:
that forever smiling damned bastard,
villain, what-have-you, is dead
and no latest success of his
can embitter our days with envy,
paralyze us into temporary impotency,
despair rotting our guts and liver;
yes, though the greatest that ever wuz
or ever will be he's dead, dead,
and all the numerous flattering busts
keep him safely nailed down
among the worms he so often went raving
on about when his great heart burst
and all the griefs of the world
came flooding out. His ghost may wander
like Caesar's into my tent
by this rented lake, and I'll entertain
him; but he must also stand outside
begging for entry when I keep his volume
shut, and then he's out in the cold
like his own poor Lear. And—well—
there's my six-year-old son
who says of the clothes flapping
on the clothesline: "Look, they're
scratching themselves," or compares
his mother's nipples to drain-plugs
he says he wishes to pull out, or
tells me the rain is air crying
– and he only four at the time;
and though I swear I never told him
of Prospero and his great magic
asked me the other day: "Is the world real?"
So who really can tell, maybe one day
one of my clan will make it
and there'll be another cock-of-the-walk,
another king-of-the-castle; anyway
we've got our bid in, Old Bard.

ARAN ISLANDS

Dun Aengus

High walls . . . of stones;
man-humbling cliff and shattering sea,
ramparts:
trenches of stone, fierce four of them
and in-between
prehistory's barbed wire, *cheveux de frise*
. . . of stones.

Enclosing a mist.

Gone are the defenders;
gone, they who attacked.

Nothing here:
only mist
and blue-grey stones.

Cliffs of Moher

At last, as in a dream,
I've come to the cliffs
from where God hurls down
his enemies, every one.

Rat-faced cunning mercers
with a rat's delight;
all, all who are dead of soul,
male and female.

See, their polls open like flowers
on the black rocks below;
their brains dance with the foam
on a green wave's tow.

Kilmurvey

Low are the hills, a mere rise
in the ground, grey with stones and green;
Stand anywhere and you can trace
outlines with your new-found eyes
of stone fences delicate as lace:
Stand anywhere and you can be seen.

INSPIRATION

I have brought you to this Greek village
famed for its honey
as others are for their bread or wine
Love-making kept us awake
half the night
afterwards the jiggers took over
and would not let us sleep
Cocks and crowing women
woke us from our troubled doze
We compared laughingly the red bruises
on our arms and cheeks
Your good mouth, as it always does,
made me drool
and my spirit rose at once
In this stupid century
addlepated professors and mechanics
decry Inspiration
Alas, their arms have never held her;
gazing at you, woman,
in this shy early morning light I could more easily
doubt the feel of the bare boards under my feet
Truly this goddess has being
– in you, in some rare almost forgotten poems
and the mountainous hills and sea
which are waiting for us to look at them,
this vinestem curling on our windowsill
this bee
Come, let us show them
the fierce lumps on our divine foreheads

THE COCKROACH

She was from Tokyo.
He was from Tabriz.
They met in a bookstore.
They both reached for the same book.
Excuse me, in Japanese.
Excuse me, in Persian.
The book was a treatise on the cockroach.
Each wanted the book.
There was only one copy.
They agreed to purchase it together.
Both were specialists in the make-up
and behaviour of cockroaches.
Fascinated lifelong students, they were.
Now they became fascinated with each other.
They fell in love looking at charts of cockroaches
ingesting whatever it is cochroaches ingest.
He took her to his apartment.
She took him to hers.
They went for long walks together.
They frequently talked about other things
besides cockroaches.
He read her his favourite Sanskrit poets.
She read him Haikus.
Examining the reproductive organs of their favourite
insect, their genitals became moist.
In his apartment; then in hers
It was delightful.
It was romantic.
They were exceedingly happy.
The affair should have lasted forever.
It brought a shine to their eyes.
It did something to their voices.
They were very tender to each other.
He brought her some verses of his own.
She had a gift for him flown in from Tokyo.
Then one day they had a disagreement.
It was over the feeding habits of the cockroach.
He said one thing, she said another.
The disagreement became an argument.
The argument became a quarrel.
The quarrel became violent and bitter.

They could not agree on the feeding habits of the cockroach.
The gulf between them grew wider and wider.
He said this, she said that.
There could be no compromise.
Only one could be right.
They hissed at each other.
Their eyes filled with hatred.
They questioned each other's intelligence and lineage.
All the lovely, meaningful things they had said to each other
about cockroaches were forgotten.
It was sad.
It was very sad.
It ended with his taking his verses back.
She told him to keep the treatise on the cockroach
since plainly he needed it more than she did.
Bitch, in Persian.
Ignorant louse, in Japanese.
So the affair ended.
It was sad.
It was very sad.

THE BARONESS

He smiles gratefully when I tell him his beard
        makes him look like Solzhenitsyn
His wife is on some other island
        screwing other men
She will join him at the end of summer
There are so many, many islands in Greece
Her man-of-science hubby directs a Munich laboratory
        hopping in and out an enormous test-tube
Each morning he has his big erection in a glass cylinder
He'd rather stare at oxides than at a woman's breasts
        and the odourlessness of bismuth really turns him on
I've seen and felt his wife's breasts
They are not made of bismuth
        and, heated, give off a rank delicious smell
Erotic missionary, I see her bringing that smell
        to the remotest parts of the Aegean
Impregnating with it the flora of the countryside
Greece will never be the same when she's through

49

Even the colonels will be sent sprawling
    on their backs: I mean that literally
With her crushing their heads between her massive thighs
    or wiping her blonde twat with their tongues for napkins
What a woman! I call her the Baroness
She's not a woman, she's a phenomenon
    especially when she dances in a ruined castle
    with no one to applaud her performance but myself
A Valkyrie in a bikini!
What a sight! Yeats would have come in his velveteen pants
    a dozen times
And Eliot flushed his poems down the nearest toilet
O these sweet English boys talking about love and women
Take it from me, English poetry when it isn't the death wish
    is voyeurism and cuntsniffing
    but done with so much aplomb you take it
    for spirituality or a concern with art and the good life
If they were alive (were they ever?) and my Baroness
    laid a magical finger on them
    they'd both shit in their pants
    and run to their wives to clean them up
Or get a Harvard professor to do it for them
When my Baroness dances in a run-down medieval castle
    I think of her man-of-science hubby
    looking green and impotent
    away from his beloved molecules
And have wild, exhilarating thoughts
    about culture and civilization
    before I take her into my arms
And complete the dance with her under the broken turrets

**RECIPE FOR A LONG
AND HAPPY LIFE**

Give all your nights
to the study of Talmud

By day practise
shooting from the hip

OSIP MANDELSHTAM (1891-1940)

I once did an hour-long TV show reading
from your *Stamen* and *Tristia*: out there
were my compatriots who had never before
heard of your name and pain, your nightmare fate;
of course the impressario spoke impressively
about your stay in Paris where you mastered
the French symbolists, your skill as translator
(what pre-Belsen Jew hadn't promiscuously
shacked up with five or six gentile cultures)
the Hellenic feeling in your prose and poems
– to be brief, he filled in the familiar picture
of enlightened Jew ass bared to the winds

But when that self-taught master symbolist
il miglior fabbro put you on his list of touchables
that was the end; you perished in the land waste
of Siberia, precisely where no one knows and few care
for in that stinking imperium whose literature
you adorned like a surrealist Star of David
you're still an unclaimed name, a Jewish ghost
who wanders occasionally into enclaves
of forelorn intellectuals listening
for the ironic scrape of your voice
in the subversive hum of underground presses

I know my fellow-Canadians, Osip;
they forgot your name and fate as swiftly
as they learned them, switching off
the contorted image of pain with their sets
choosing a glass darkness to one which starting
in the mind covers the earth in permanent eclipse;
so they chew branflakes and crabmeat gossip make love
take out insurance against fires and death
while our poetesses explore their depressions
in delicate complaints regular as menstruation
or eviscerate a dead god for metaphors;
the men-poets displaying codpieces of wampum,
the safer legends of prairie Indian and Eskimo

Under a sour and birdless heaven
TV crosses stretch across a flat Calvary
and plaza storewindows give me
the blank expressionless stare of imbeciles:
this is Toronto, not St. Petersburg on the Neva;
though seas death and silent decades separate us
we yet speak to each other, brother to brother;
your forgotten martyrdom has taught me scorn
for hassidic world-savers without guns and tanks:
they are mankind's gold and ivory toilet bowls
where brute or dictator relieves himself
when reading their grave messages to posterity
– let us be the rapturous eye of the hurricane
flashing the Jew's will, his mocking contempt for slaves

LILLIAN ROXON

Asthmatic and always stuffing your face;
Your lymph glands brimming with chemicals to control
Unavailingly your adiposity and sinister wheezings;
The sudden breathlessness that threatened each time
To unhook your fat body from your soul. . . .

You've taken the whole works into the grave
With you. After all the noisy convulsive shakes
Like those of a resistless locomotive rumbling
Out of the station – silence. Uncanny silence.
Not a single wheeze can ever startle you awake.

Death, the fathead, struck you when you were alone;
Stabbed that great heart of yours, sparing
The mediocrities and prudent losers your scorned.
So many lumps to choose from, their numbers increasing,
And that dull jerk must come and strike you down.

My dear incomparable Lilli, I find it strange to think
I shall never hear again your indecorous wit
Or see your wide luminous eyes glitter with humour
And affection. Unencumbered, now lighter than air
My fat companionable pole-vaulter, you leave the ground
and soar.

THE VENTRILOQUIST

The brightly painted puppets
are in their places again:

Smiling to one another
over the butchered meat of cows and sheep
the spiced legs and wings of braised chicken
talking chortling crowing
blinking their eyes in affection
or good humour, cracking jokes
and giving each other sly digs
to put the table in an uproar of merriment

To add to the realism
the pink-faced waiters are perspiring
the manager wearing frown and black gaberdine
hurries towards the solitary diner
and the radio plays a Mendelssohn *lied*

In a far corner of the restaurant
two shadowy figures at set intervals
move the Gothic chess pieces across a board
as if they were miniature landmines

And at a given signal
the six card-players stop their game
to argue hotly the political news of the day:
the brutal killing of a party leader
of surprising astuteness
and manoeuvrability

Unexpectedly I overhear from another table
someone say I adore you Lisl, I love you Lisl
and a puppet in slacks and purple blouse
murmur sadly I love you too Heinrich

Though I look everywhere for him
the diabolical ventriloquist
is nowhere to be seen

ADAM

I wish we could go back
to the beginning

when there were no hospitals
and no churches dispensing
the analgesics of religion,
not even the famous eye-tingling one
in Milan, the *Il Duomo*;
no typewriters furiously clicking out
for the jocoseness of cherubs and angels
our latest humiliation and impotency;
when there were no circus freaks
Fellini freaks, speedfreaks, Jesusfreaks
no Seventh Day Adventists, Scientologists
apocalyptics, epileptics, eupeptics, and skeptics
and no bloated greedyguts
stuffing their diseased bladders
with paper money and gold,
no courtesans lining their perfumed orifices
with expensive many-hued crystals
amassed at Cusy's

Before the human larnyx acquired
its tinge of querulous dissatisfaction
and mind became a forever open wound
of militant self-serving cynicism and doubt
Before Caesar crossed the Rubicon
because there was no Rubicon to cross
and no Alexander the Dardanelles
because there was no Dardanelles
and no Alexander handsome and mad;
no Darius, no Sarpedon, no Xerxes
no Pharaohs, no Baals, no Astarte
no Chinese dynasties or ideograms
nurturing in their mysterious script
Maoism and the Long March

There's only God and myself
in the cool first evening in Eden
discussing his fantastic creation,
the moon and the stars,
and the enveloping stillness.
About the woman
he has in mind for me
we talk softly and for a long time
and very, very carefully.

THE SHARK

In some quiet bay
or deserted inlet
he is waiting for me.

It is noon
there is a stillness on water and land
as if some primal god is about to speak;
in the sky
not a single bird is to be seen flying

I shall swim out towards him
bringing him my incurable moral ache
and my cancered liver,
memories of women laughter Greek islands
griefs and humiliations I could find no words for

I want him to be black, wholly black
I want him to be famished and solitary
I want him to be quietly ready for me
as if he were the angel of death

The last thing I want my alive eyes
to behold before I close them forever
are his ripsaw teeth.

BLACKOUT

Suddenly everyone feels
weightless as a whisper
                        unreal
and drained of substantiality;
most pitiful seem the children,
pointless as their own queries

The restaurant is lit
by tiny candleflares on each table;
the shadows flickering on the wall
could be Turks advancing or retreating,
Achilles' spear, the greaves of Ajax

The scene is as old as man's ferocity;
so is the scarcely concealed excitement
at the approach of catastrophe,
the prospect of something unusual
about to happen
                        to confer meaning
on lives otherwise meaningless
and without glory

O Habbakuk
slide down from your heavenly terebinth
convince us
                huddled around this martial box
it is punishment for some sin
done out of anger or pride:
come, make our possible deaths
welcome and intelligible

This day
a hundred handsome young Greeks
a hundred handsome young Turks
had their blood spilled out
like so much slop

SEDUCTION OF AND BY A CIVILIZED FRENCHWOMAN

Having agreed that Simone de Beauvoir's feminism
is a bad joke
that Sartre is a has-been and a stupid
Jansenist muddlehead
that Camus possessed more integrity than talent
that there are no longer any poets in France
worth mentioning
that much the same could be said for her novelists
and that, in general, French culture
is in a parlous condition, if not actually dead
not having cared to move
a single centimetre beyond Flaubert and Valery
and that no one except the two of us
seemed to know what is happening to that wretched country
having agreed politely to disagree
about Hemingway, Rimbaud, Holderlin, Nietzsche, Brecht,
Lawrence, Moravia, Jaspers, Kafka, Strindberg, and Pasternak's
Dr. Zhivago having dismissed politics as a *bêtise* and religion
as a *folie*

AND

Having inevitably but cautiously left the high ground
of literary and philosophical discussion
to speak of more personal, more mundane matters
i.e. one's dissatisfactions with conventional marriage, one's
adulteries, fornications, venereal diseases (there were none)
and given a description of the circumstances attendant on one's
best and worst fucks
having slyly dropped two or three hints
about one's favourite erogenous zones and the best means
for stimulating them
and having led from this to the over-riding, paramount need in
sex for tenderness, mutual esteem, humour, *délicatesse* and for
similar though not necessarily identical tastes in literature, music,
philosophy, art, theatre, and contemporary films
 we are now ready to make love

FOR MY BROTHER JESUS

My father had terrible words for you
– whoreson, bastard, *meshumad*;
and my mother loosed Yiddish curses
on your name and the devil's spawn
on their way to church
that scraped the frosted horsebuns
from the wintry Montreal street
to fling clattering into our passageway

Did you ever hear an angered
Jewish woman curse? Never mind the words:
at the intonations alone, Jesus,
the rusted nails would drop out
from your pierced hands and feet
and scatter to the four ends of earth

Luckless man, at least
that much you were spared

In my family you
were a *mamzer*, a *yoshke pondrick*
and main reason for their affliction and pain.
Even now I see the contemptuous curl
on my gentle father's lips;
my mother's never-ending singsong curses
still ring in my ears more loud
than the bells I heard each Sunday morning,
their clappers darkening the outside air

Priests and nuns
were black blots on the snow
– forbidding birds, crows

Up there
up there beside the Good Old Man
we invented and the lyring angels
do you get the picture, my hapless brother:
deserted daily, hourly
by the Philistines you hoped to save
and the murdering heathens,
your own victimized kin hating and despising
you?

O crucified poet
your agonized face haunts me
as it did when I was a boy;
I follow your strange figure
through all the crooked passageways
of history, the walls reverberating
with ironic whisperings and cries,
the unending sound of cannonfire
and rending groans, the clatter
of bloodsoaked swords falling
on armour and stone
to lose you finally among your excited brethren
haranguing and haloing them
with your words of love,
your voice gentle as my father's

PARQUE DE MONTJUICH

I

In European cemeteries my brothers lie
neither ignored nor neglected; they cause
not even a tremor of shame or embarrassment
but if sometimes thought of, thought of then
as something heteroclite – even intriguing –
like a freakish trinket whose origin has been forgotten

How clean-smelling, how green and fertile
this park, once a Jewish cemetery
where they hauled in the broken bones from the nearby ghetto;
One wonders, standing beside these shrubs, these trees,
did the grass come up cleaner, darker
for marrow and flesh being occasionally toasted

Yet, look! Beyond the tourist museums Columbus,
in his molten arms the blood of Marranos,
proudly turns his back on the cathedrals and whores;
standing high above the city on his astrolabe
he points his raised finger to the New World
beyond these foul streets, the polluted stinking harbours

II

Prickly as the Jews whose dust they cover
these grotesque misshapen cacti
climb the hot and dusty mountainsides

They cluster in green squalid ghettos
contorting like Hebrew letters some hand dispersed
upon this arid, inhospitable ground

Between them, catching at once mind and eye
the vidid perennial blood-drops of geraniums
that thrive, their stems cut again and again

While towering above red flowers, cacti and rock
brood the dark rabbinical cypresses
giving coolth and dignity to their anguished flock

III

I sit on the weatherbeaten bench. Before me
the busy harbour; yet all that I can see
are the round-roofed steel sheds and cranes
between stone pillars making a perfect
focus for my dazzled eyes. They select
the sheer lines rising grey and plain
that tilt in all directions starkly
as if in abstract collusion with the cacti
my gaze takes in on either side
each time I turn my marvelling head

Yet here where each bloom is green or red
where botanists might feel wholly glad
to touch exotic shrubs, flowers, towering palmtrees
I see clearly framed between those pillars now
the black phylactery box on my father's brow
blotting out nature's joyful variety;
smell below these neatly parterred stones
the detritus of long-forgotten flesh and bones
and hear all morning no other sound
but Rachel's voice rising from the ground

SURVIVOR

If at first it disgusts you
be a man: don't give up, don't despair
in this as in most things
habit and practice make perfect

In the beginning try only
for small effects, small incisions
leave the big spurts
for a later period

Start by imagining
an eyeball in your hand
intact as yet, still warm
now put its fellow beside it

In the beginning was the deed:
give yourself a year, no more
to have real eyeballs in your hand
make sure you wipe the blade clean afterward

Continue to read poems
and to enjoy wit in conversation
motto for our times: cultivate your tastes
but deaden your senses

At the beginning if you're careless
feelings may trip you up
you must unlearn tenderness and compassion
above all, compassion

Let all your reveries be of charred bodies
of smashed blue faces
it's not simple
but it's not that difficult either

O JERUSALEM

Jerusalem, you will be betrayed again and again:
not by the brave young men who die for you
with military cries on their blue lips
—never by these
                    And never by the scholars
who know each sunken goat-track
that winds somehow into your legend, your great name
and not by those dreamers
                              who looking for the beginnings
of your strange wizardry ascend from storied darkness
holding dust and warped harps in their blistered hands

These will always find you and bring you
offerings of blood and bone
                              lowering their grave eyes
as to an idol made neither of wood nor stone   .
nor brick nor any metal
                    yet clearly visible
as though sitting on a jewelled throne
                              O Jerusalem
you are too pure and break men's hearts
you are a dream of prophets, not for our clay,
and drive men mad by your promised
impossible peace, your harrowing oracles of love;
and how may we walk upon this earth
                              with forceful human stir
unless we adore you and betray?

FOR MY DISTANT WOMAN

I remember you as you were in Paxi,
my distant woman, and send my disconsolate thoughts
handspringing backwards like a clown eager for plaudits
to pick up your scents again, your smiles, your tenderness.

Agile and talented, he will never catch up with you
though to nudge him harder I've promised him top billing
in a floodlighted arena of his own choosing:
not even the cleverest dog could pick up your scent again.

My absent darling, fragrance and tenderness are strewn
on the silver ripples we both watched one night
when the full moon and all the stars were listening to us:
they cling to whispers beyond the reach of dog and clown.

Your blurring image enters my nostalgia softly
as the sun's semen enters the crimson flowercup
and often, as now, like the first heavy gout of rain
that makes it toss and shiver on its tender stem.

POLE-VAULTER

Now that grey fluff
covers my chest
and it's the glasses on my nose
that sparkle, not my eyes
what the horny girls
                    want from me
is advice on
how to allure young men;
                            those
with ideas in their head
and pimples on their ass,
my final opinion
on the Theaetetus

They say at my age
I should be guru or sage,
not foolishly behave
like passion's slave

Ignorant trulls
in a cold land;
age will dry their flesh
and wrinkle it with useless folds.
Spry and drugged with love
I pole-vault
                over my grave

Contents